Twenty Healthy Bean Based Sauces

Including Suggested Meal Plans

By: David Trimboli

Publisher: Red Falcon Press

Disclaimer

This book does not intend in any way to treat, cure, or prevent any disease or medical condition. If you are on medication, have a medical condition or are pregnant or nursing always consult your physician before changing your diet. It is the responsibility of the user to avoid ingredients that they may be allergic to. The author will not be held liable for food allergy reactions or any effects of eating spoiled or improperly prepared foods. If you use this book you acknowledge your understanding and accept the items in this disclaimer.

Cover Graphics, Logo and Photography by: David Trimboli
Illustrations were purchased and used with permission.

Red Falcon Press

DEDICATION

This book is dedicated to two of my maternal great great uncles. Genealogy research is still incomplete, but one is most likely named Giovanni DeNuntis, the other's name is not known to me. My mother conveyed that they were both professional chefs. Born as twins in Italy, one stayed to practice there, and the other one moved to practice his skill in France. They were probably born in about the 1870's and maybe practiced their craft in about the 1890's and forward.

Chapter	Title	Page
1	Introduction	1
2	Required Tools	5
3	Cleaning and Cooking the Dried Beans	9
4	Using Canned Beans	13
5	Sauce Creation Method (For All Recipes)	14
6	Sauce Recipes	23
	Kidney Cumin	24
	Garbanzo Basil	26
	Lentil Coriander	28
	Garbanzo Clove	30
	Pinto Basil	32
	Garbanzo Oregano	34
	Cannellini Coriander	36
	Black Cardamom	38
	Lentil Clove	40
	Cannellini Rosemary	42
	Garbanzo Rosemary	44
	Cannellini Basil	46

Garbanzo Pinto Basil   48

Kidney Oregano   50

Kidney Black Cumin   52

Lima Basil   54

Kidney Rosemary   56

Pinto Dill   58

Cannellini Tarragon   60

Pinto Black Basil   62

7   Serving and Variations   64

8   Sauce Storage   66

9   Example Meals for the Sauces   67

10 Food Index   73

ACKNOWLEDGMENTS

I invented and developed these sauces mostly on my own. I did get an occasional suggestion that I used from a colleague or friend. I want to thank Prathibha Prabhakaran and Zulfikar Ali for suggestions about the sauce creation.

Editors include: Patricia Pats Gurin, Gale Neal, and Jennifer Vogh.

Serving Advice: Connie Camillo

1 INTRODUCTION

I am writing this book to share some healthy bean-based sauces that I have invented. I am hoping that people find them both flavorful and healthy. My three most important criteria for creating the sauces were that they should be: sustaining, very healthy and have good flavor. Two other important requirements are that they should be easy to make and storable for 2 to 4 days in the refrigerator. The story behind how and why they were developed will be described next.

I worked in the very technically demanding fields of mechanical design and engineering for 34 years. During this time, I had many problems with blood sugar stability. The blood sugar drops would manifest at random times during the day, I would experience fatigue, brain fog and even lightheadedness. Two or three times a week it would become so severe that I felt like I might pass out. I believe that this was caused by the fact that I am hypoglycemic combined with the intense mental activity required to perform this type of work. I finally solved some of this problem with a special breakfast in 2007; however, there was still significant room for improvement. So, my next research would go into designing a lunch that would better sustain me through the day.

I developed a base meal consisting of lettuce, rice, vegetables and meat. The types of ingredients used in these meals were constantly varied so as not to get boring. I tend to eat very healthy using whole organic foods. These were working pretty well but they still needed something more. That is when I started looking for sauces to make the meals more sustaining and interesting. I tried vinegar and oil which was not too bad but the vinegar does not really complement the meat and rice so well. Also, there are no sustaining properties to the vinegar and oil. Then there was the tomato sauce phase which did not last too long before I abandoned them. I tried regular spaghetti tomato sauces, tomato paste by itself and the jarred diced tomatoes. Boiling down broth-based sauces to thicken them was tried as well but that did not work well for me either. So far none of these sauces were working very well. I was looking for something that would be generally applicable to all of the base meal variations that I had developed. I tried a few other purchased products that were also unsuccessful; I was really beginning to feel that I was not going to have any success in this endeavor. In this frustrated state and almost ready to give up I decided to rely on and trust my own judgment. This is where I had the idea to use puréed beans as the base.

My first bean-based sauces were created in September of 2013. I invented a new sauce every week for approximately two years giving me a base of over 100 sauces to work with. I eventually went back and started modifying and improving some of them. These first sauces were created with canned beans. But after doing some research I discovered that some of the liners inside the cans may have some health issues. Due to this and advice from a colleague I found that dried beans both taste better and are healthier. Therefore, I decided to use dried beans exclusively. In the course of development of these sauces, I started with single bean-based recipes and just a few spices. Although simple, some of these first sauces turned out very well. As this process matured I started blending more spices and incorporated combinations of different beans as well. I am still tinkering with these sauces today over four years later. Throughout this process, I kept a very detailed logbook on what I tried. I documented carefully what worked well and what did not.

The general meal type that I use incorporates a bed of lettuce, some rice, vegetables, meat and of course the sauce. Immediately after the first couple of recipes created in 2013, I noticed a significant difference in how well I felt after lunch. Since they are very hearty there is a brief lull in energy. After that, I found that they sustained my blood sugar very well through the rest of the afternoon. Being very hearty these meals are also exceptional for fall and winter.

I want to be very clear that I am not making any general medical claims about this sauce being good for the hypoglycemic state. I can only say how it worked for me.

These sauces have a very wide range of application and are compatible with many meal types. I will provide some example meals that I prefer at the end of the book to use the sauces with.

Also, note that none of these recipes include salt. It is left up to the cook to salt to taste. Or, you can leave it up to each individual to salt to taste on their plate.

The following paragraph is very general and for information only. I am being very careful to not make any specific health claims. I will share some reasons as to why I am using some of the ingredients. I am only sharing this information to give the reader a starting point to read and further investigate on their own.

Turmeric is used in all of the recipes because I have read of its many health benefits. The claims about the reducing brain fog and mental fatigue, were very interesting. It is widely used and there are many documents on its properties. I believe that the beans and oils used have good nutritional properties. The oils and the beans will also provide some omega-9, omega-6 and omega-3 fatty acids. I do believe they are not prominent in large amounts but nonetheless, they are a source. From what I have read I believe the omega-3 fatty acids are the most important. The beans are also a good source of fiber and protein.

These sauces can be enjoyed by people with many types of diets.

2 REQUIRED TOOLS

Below you will find a list of items required to make the sauce.

1) You will need a measuring scale that reads out in grams or ounces (see figure 1). There are many products on the market and any device is fine. Just make sure it can handle the combined weight of the containers and food you are measuring.

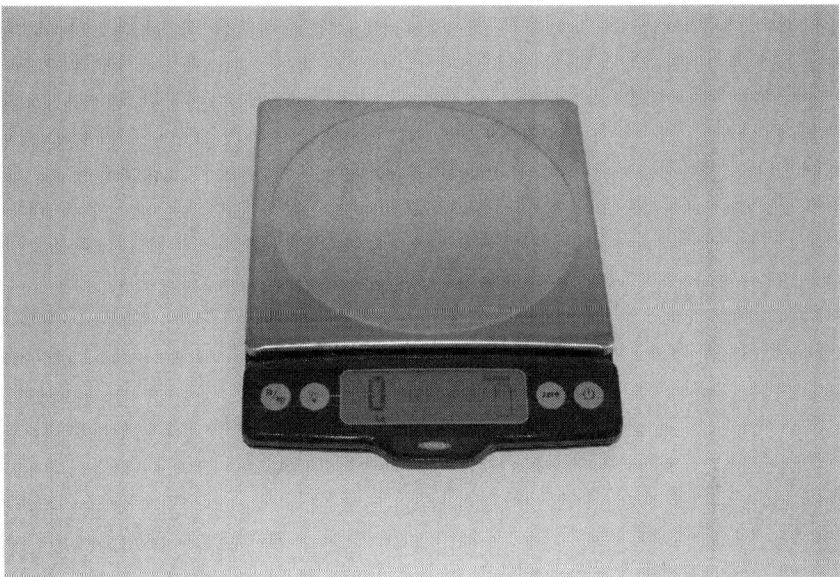

Figure 1 Weight Scale

2) You will also need a saucepan with a lid. For this application, a 2-quart saucepan works very well (see figure 2).

Figure 2 Two Quart Stainless Steel Saucepan

3) English or metric measuring spoons are also a necessity. Some spoons have English units but also show the metric equivalent (see figure 3).

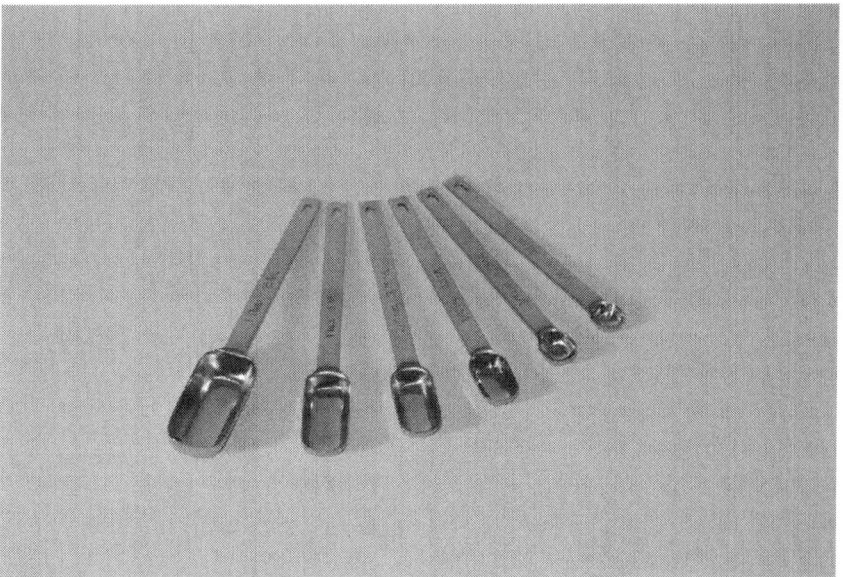

Figure 3 Measuring Spoons (English / Metric Units)

4) You will need a blender or food processor. Any product will do that has sufficient power. A 400 W machine will work sufficiently for some sauces but you will sometimes have to thin the mixture out with water to get it to blend properly.

The Vitamix 7500 shown in figure 4 is one of the more powerful machines for home use. This is a 1640 W machine (2.2 horsepower) and does very well for all of the sauces. With this in mind, a blender or food processor between 800 and 1640 W is best. Wattages are typically shown on all machines.

Figure 4 Blender or Food Processor (Vitamix Shown)

5) Choose a container for the final sauce with 3 cups or greater volume. This container should have an airtight lid. Glass containers are preferred because sometimes the taste of plastic can leach into the sauce. Plastic lids are okay.

3 CLEANING AND COOKING THE DRIED BEANS

1) In this section, you will learn the process of cooking/soaking the beans.
2) Choose a recipe and make sure that you have all of the ingredients.
3) Then measure out the dried beans by weight (see figure 5) and inspect them for any foreign matter or spoiled beans.

Figure 5 Measuring the Beans

4) (It is good to add an extra three or four beans of each type to test their cooking state periodically.) A 2-quart saucepan is just about ideal but you can use what you like. Fill the pan with enough water to totally submerge all of the beans. Scrub the beans with your hands. Do this by grabbing the beans in your palm and rub them underwater between your fingers and palm (see figure 6).

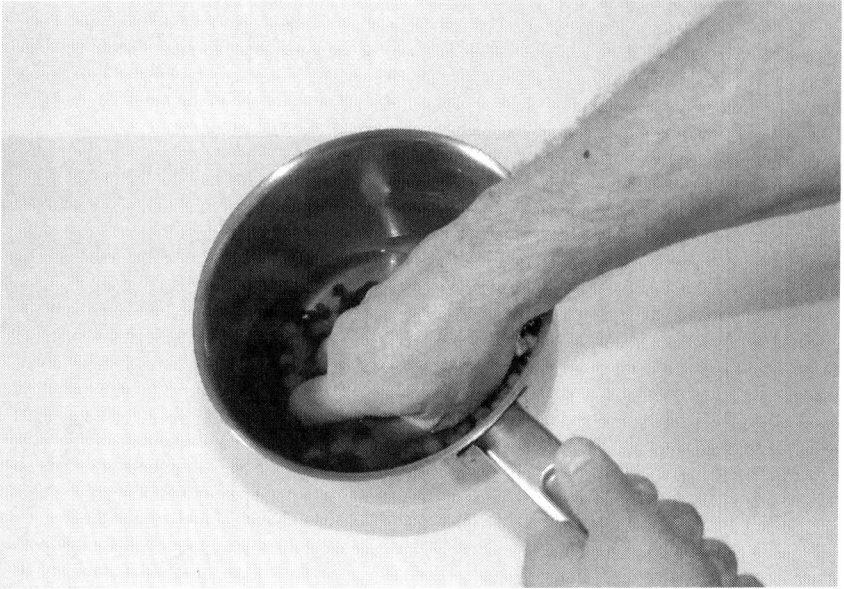

Figure 6 Washing the Beans

Then pour off the water. This is required to remove any dirt that was not washed away during packaging. Do this at least twice or until you are satisfied that they are clean.

5) There are many ways of soaking/cooking beans. If you have a preferred method you can use that. Whichever method you choose, make sure that your beans are in an edible state before making the sauce. This is why you put in a few extra beans. When you think they are cooked enough, chew one bean of each type to make sure they are soft and ready-to-eat.

6) The following is the preferred cooking/soaking method. Once you are satisfied that the beans are clean, pour three cups of fresh water into the saucepan. The beans should be totally submerged with at least one inch of water over the top of the beans. Place the saucepan on a stove with no

lid and bring the water to a boil. Then turn the burner off and put the lid on the pan. Do not boil the beans with the lid on because they can easily boil over if left unattended. Let the beans soak in the hot water for about one-half hour then pour this water out. Rinse the beans and then add three more cups of water. Without the lid on, bring the beans and water to a boil once more. If you like you can place a dash of salt in the water. Put the lid back on the pan and let it sit for three hours. Make sure the burner is off during the soaking time.

After three hours remove the lid and bring the water to a boil once more. Turn off the burner and place the lid back on the pan. Let the pan set for another three hours. After six hours of cooking chew a bean of each type to see if they are thoroughly soaked/cooked (see figure 7).

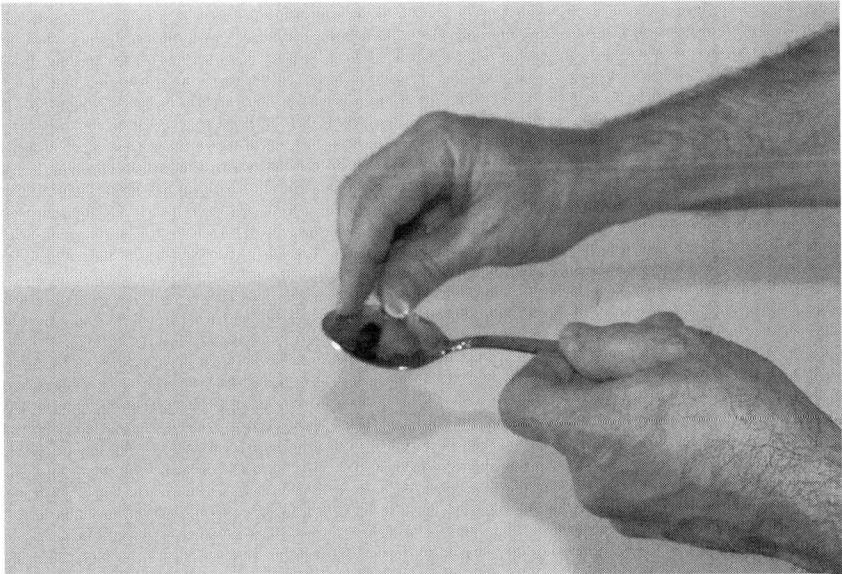

Figure 7 Test Beans by Chewing One of Each Type

If they are tender and edible your soaking is complete. If not, repeat the boiling and 3-hour soak process as needed and test again. If desired you can append this process with an overnight soak. After you are satisfied that the beans have been soaked properly, drain the water and rinse the beans once more. Note that different types of beans require different cooking times. For example, garbanzo beans take much longer to soak than lentils. To avoid overcooking/soaking you can put the lentils in before the last boiling process.

During the cooking/soaking process make sure that the beans are always submerged and never leave the heat on during soaking. Also, do not use the pan lid whenever bringing the mixture to a boil.

4 USING CANNED BEANS

If you have decided to make your sauce using canned beans, the guidelines below will help you to decide how to purchase and process them.

The first thing to understand is that a 15 ounce can of beans does not contain 15 ounces of beans. The total 15-ounce net weight is the measurement of the beans and the water. A current Consumer Report article claims that the food content ranges between 52% and 66% actual food. This means that in your 15 ounce can of beans only 8 to 10 ounces will be actual food. The rest is water.

So, when planning your purchase for canned beans assume that you have about 8 ounces of beans in a 15 ounce can to be conservative.

Each recipe is laid out on two pages (see chapter 6). The page to the right has a table showing the required amounts for canned beans. The table on the left-hand page is for dried beans.

After you have purchased your beans, open the can and drain the water. Then rinse the beans and weigh out the appropriate amount for the recipe you are making. Proceed directly to chapter 5 to make the sauce.

5 SAUCE CREATION METHOD (FOR ALL RECIPES)

Note that this chapter only describes the method of creating a sauce. Any pictures of ingredients are for illustration only. You will find the actual sauce recipes in chapter 6. <u>You will use this method for all of the recipes.</u>

1) After the beans have cooled to room temperature you are ready to make the sauce. Drain the water and put the pan aside for a moment.
2) Next measure the oils required for the recipe you are making and pour that into the blender (see figure 8).

Figure 8 Measuring the Oil Required

Continue by measuring the spices required and put them in the blender on top of the oil (see figures 9 - 10).

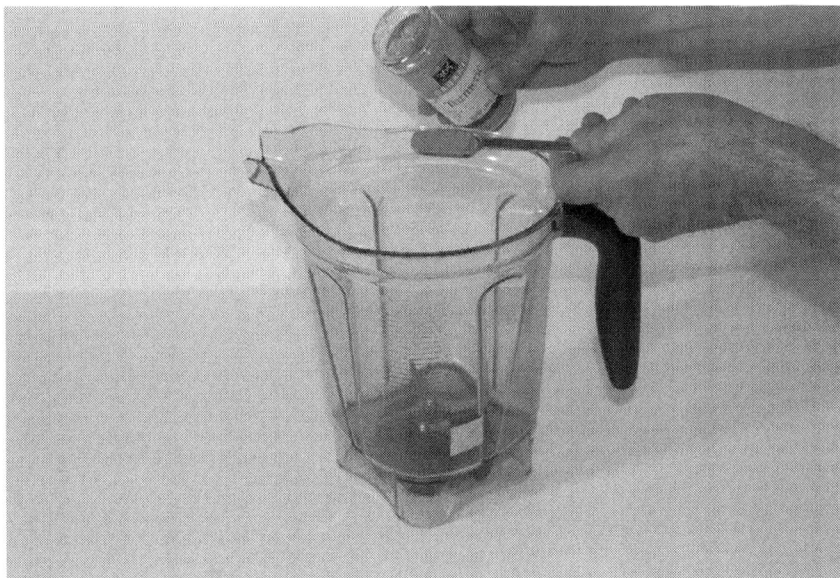

Figure 9 Measure the Spices Required

3) It is important to put the spices in after the oil because it allows them to mix more thoroughly into the sauce.

Figure 10 Spices Shown on Top of the Oil

4) Pour the beans into the blender on top of the oil and spices (see figure 11). Then add fresh water until the total volume present is 20 ounces or 2 ½ cups (see figures 12 – 13). This is the total yield of all of the sauces.

Figure 11 Pour the Cooked Beans into the Blender

Figure 12 Add Water to the 2 1/2 Cup Line

Figure 13 Total Volume of Beans, Oil, Water and Spices is 2 1/2 cups

5) A Vitamix blender is what I use, directions based on this device are given first.
   a. Make sure the blender is on the lowest speed (1) prior to turning it on (see figure 14).
   b. Turn on the blender and then turn the speed dial to maximum (10) slowly over the course of about six or seven seconds.

Figure 14 Blending the Sauce

   c. Then immediately do the same in reverse turning the speed dial from maximum to minimum over the course of about six or seven seconds. The results are shown in figure 15.

Figure 15 The Blended Sauce

6) For some sauces with softer bean types (like lentils), this will be enough. You do not want to over blend them because the sauce will have no texture. Over blended sauces will have the consistency of a peanut butter. This takes away from the appetizing nature of the sauce. Always lightly blend it at first so that it is thick and grainy. You can always blend more finely, but start out coarse because you cannot go back (see figures 16 – 17).

Figure 16 The Completed Sauce

Figure 17 The Texture of the Sauce

7) Note that a very chunky sauce will cause the sauce to separate. Separation means that some of the water and oil will pool on the top of the sauce. It will take some practice to get the right consistency for your taste. If you prefer a chunkier sauce that is ok you can just stir before serving.

8) Once you have a sauce that has the granular size that you like it still may be too thick. If so, decant the sauce into a storage or serving container. To thin the sauce, add a tablespoon or so of water at a time and stir it in briskly with a spoon. Work this process slowly so as not to over dilute the mixture. I prefer a tiny bit chunky sauce with a moderately thick consistency (see Figure 17). Over time you will fine-tune these skills and develop a sauce thickness and granularity that suits you.

9) For other blender types, use a similar process and index the speed up in whatever manner your device allows. For example, if it is a pushbutton selection for speed then progressively start at a lower speed and work your way up. The durations for blending times using the Vitamix will not pertain to your device. Since the Vitamix machine is very powerful, it is likely that your blending times will need to be longer. Therefore, it may take a little experimentation to get the process to work. To compensate for a lower power blender, you can begin with 25% of the beans and add the rest in slowly so as not to overload your device. Adding water to this process will also help. Be aware that a little bit of water goes a long way so you will want to add it a tablespoon at a time. The bottom line is the granular texture that you achieve. If you get what you want, the blender power and process is not so important.

10) And that is all that is to it. If you are using it immediately you can spoon it on your food as desired. If you are going to use it later, pour the sauce into a sealable container and place it in the refrigerator. These sauces will normally last about 2 to 4 days in the refrigerator, however, they can also be frozen if you desire.

Note that on each recipe page the units for the recipe are listed in both English and metric units. Use only one of these columns, not both.

Also, no salt amounts are listed in the recipes. This was done purposefully so you will need to salt to taste for your liking.

When you have spices that are very tough like Rosemary you may wish to pre-chop it on a cutting board to make sure it blends in thoroughly.

What if you want 5 cups of sauce instead of 2 ½ ? It is best to just repeat the process twice at 2 ½ cups as it is not much extra work. This research, process development and method was conducted at a 2 ½ cup blend. So to be successful it may be a good idea to only make it in 2 ½ cup amounts. If you are making more than 2 ½ cups, you can however cook all of the beans at once to save some time.

6 SAUCE RECIPES

In this chapter, you will find the actual sauce recipes. As you open to each recipe you will find the same recipe on adjacent pages. The page to the left always has the recipe for using dried beans, and the page on the right has the exact same recipe if you are using canned beans. To make a recipe you will use either page never both.

The page on the left will refer you to chapters 3 and 5 describing the process to make the sauce from dried beans. The page on the right will refer you to chapters 4 and 5 describing the process to make the sauce from canned beans. Just to be perfectly clear chapters 3, 4 and 5 are strictly methods and contain no ingredients.

If you will be serving all of the sauce in one sitting, you can use dried or fresh herbs. If you will be storing the sauce, dried herbs are recommended.

Once you understand the methods in chapters 3, 4 and 5 you will probably not need to refer back to them again as they are very straightforward. Reading them at least once is recommended to understand the technique.

Kidney Cumin (Using Dried Beans)

If you are using dried beans use the table below. Refer to chapters 3 and 5 for the method.

Bean Type	English Ounces	Metric Grams
Kidney	4 1/4	120

Oils	Tablespoons	Milliliters
Sesame	4	60

Spices	Teaspoons	Milliliters
Turmeric	1	5
Marjoram	1/2	2
Cumin	1/2	2
Thyme	1/2	2

Try with Example Meal 1 (Chapter 9)

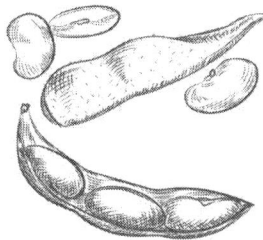

Kidney Cumin (Using Canned Beans)

If you are using canned beans use the table below. Refer to chapters 4 and 5 for the method.

Bean Type	English Ounces	Metric Grams
Kidney (No Liquid)	9 5/8	270

Oils	Tablespoons	Milliliters
Sesame	4	60

Spices	Teaspoons	Milliliters
Turmeric	1	5
Marjoram	1/2	2
Cumin	1/2	2
Thyme	1/2	2

Try with Example Meal 1 (Chapter 9)

Garbanzo Basil (Using Dried Beans)

If you are using dried beans use the table below. Refer to chapters 3 and 5 for the method.

Bean Type	English Ounces	Metric Grams
Garbanzo	4 1/4	120

Oils	Tablespoons	Milliliters
Olive	4	60

Spices	Teaspoons	Milliliters
Coriander	1/2	2
Turmeric	1	5
Basil	2	10

Try with Example Meal 7 (Chapter 9)

Garbanzo Basil (Using Canned Beans)

If you are using canned beans use the table below. Refer to chapters 4 and 5 for the method.

Bean Type	English Ounces	Metric Grams
Garbanzo (No Liquid)	9 5/8	270

Oils	Tablespoons	Milliliters
Olive	4	60

Spices	Teaspoons	Milliliters
Coriander	1/2	2
Turmeric	1	5
Basil	2	10

Try with Example Meal 7 (Chapter 9)

Lentil Coriander (Using Dried Beans)

If you are using dried beans use the table below. Refer to chapters 3 and 5 for the method.

Bean Type	English Ounces	Metric Grams
Green Lentil	4 1/4	120

Oils	Tablespoons	Milliliters
Sesame	3	44
Grape Seed	1	15

Spices	Teaspoons	Milliliters
Turmeric	1	5
Coriander	1/2	2
Cumin	1/2	2

Try with Example Meal 3 (Chapter 9)

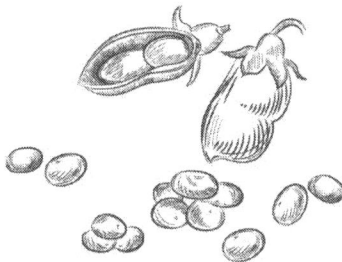

Lentil Coriander (Using Canned Beans)

If you are using canned beans use the table below. Refer to chapters 4 and 5 for the method.

Bean Type	English Ounces	Metric Grams
Green Lentil (No Liquid)	9 5/8	270

Oils	Tablespoons	Milliliters
Sesame	3	44
Grape Seed	1	15

Spices	Teaspoons	Milliliters
Turmeric	1	5
Coriander	1/2	2
Cumin	1/2	2

Try with Example Meal 3 (Chapter 9)

Garbanzo Clove (Using Dried Beans)

If you are using dried beans use the table below. Refer to chapters 3 and 5 for the method.

Bean Type	English Ounces	Metric Grams
Garbanzo	4 1/4	120

Oils	Tablespoons	Milliliters
Olive	4	60
Coconut	1 1/2	22

Spices	Teaspoons	Milliliters
Turmeric	1	5
Clove (ground)	1/2	2
Basil	3/4	4

Try with Example Meal 10 (Chapter 9)

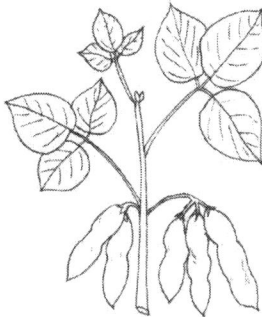

Garbanzo Clove (Using Canned Beans)

If you are using canned beans use the table below. Refer to chapters 4 and 5 for the method.

Bean Type	English Ounces	Metric Grams
Garbanzo (No Liquid)	9 5/8	270

Oils	Tablespoons	Milliliters
Olive	4	60
Coconut	1 1/2	22

Spices	Teaspoons	Milliliters
Turmeric	1	5
Cloves (ground)	1/2	2
Basil	3/4	4

Try with Example Meal 10 (Chapter 9)

Pinto Basil (Using Dried Beans)

If you are using dried beans use the table below. Refer to chapters 3 and 5 for the method.

Bean Type	English Ounces	Metric Grams
Pinto	4 1/4	120

Oils	Tablespoons	Milliliters
Safflower	4	60

Spices	Teaspoons	Milliliters
Turmeric	1	5
Basil	2	10
Coriander	1/2	2
Rosemary	3	15
Mustard (powder)	1	5

Try with Example Meal 2 (Chapter 9)

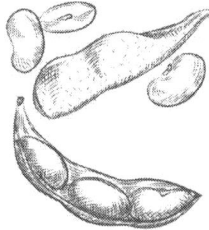

Pinto Basil (Using Canned Beans)

If you are using canned beans use the table below. Refer to chapters 4 and 5 for the method.

Bean Type	English Ounces	Metric Grams
Pinto (No Liquid)	9 5/8	270

Oils	Tablespoons	Milliliters
Safflower	4	60

Spices	Teaspoons	Milliliters
Turmeric	1	5
Basil	2	10
Coriander	1/2	2
Rosemary	3	15
Mustard (powder)	1	5

Try with Example Meal 2 (Chapter 9)

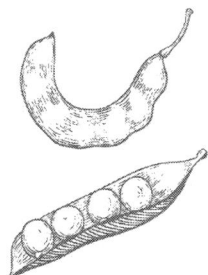

Garbanzo Oregano (Using Dried Beans)

If you are using dried beans use the table below. Refer to chapters 3 and 5 for the method.

Bean Type	English Ounces	Metric Grams
Garbanzo	2 1/4	64
Black	2 1/4	64

Oils	Tablespoons	Milliliters
Avocado	4	60

Spices	Teaspoons	Milliliters
Turmeric	1	5
Marjoram	1	5
Oregano	1	5
Tarragon	1/2	2

Try with Example Meal 4 (Chapter 9)

Garbanzo Oregano (Using Canned Beans)

If you are using canned beans use the table below. Refer to chapters 4 and 5 for the method.

Bean Type	English Ounces	Metric Grams
Garbanzo (No Liquid)	5	140
Black (No Liquid)	5	140

Oil	Tablespoons	Milliliters
Avocado	4	60

Spices	Teaspoons	Milliliters
Turmeric	1	5
Marjoram	1	5
Oregano	1	5
Tarragon	1/2	2

Try with Example Meal 4 (Chapter 9)

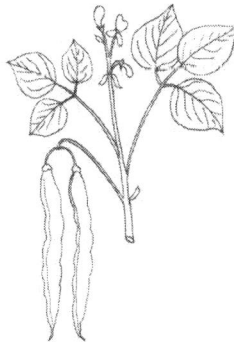

Cannellini Coriander (Using Dried Beans)

If you are using dried beans use the table below. Refer to chapters 3 and 5 for the method.

Bean Type	English Ounces	Metric Grams
Cannellini	4 1/4	120

Oils	Tablespoons	Milliliters
Olive	4	60

Spices	Teaspoons	Milliliters
Turmeric	1	5
Coriander	1 1/2	7

Try with Example Meal 5 (Chapter 9)

Cannellini Coriander (Using Canned Beans)

If you are using canned beans use the table below. Refer to chapters 4 and 5 for the method.

Bean Type	English Ounces	Metric Grams
Cannellini (No Liquid)	9 5/8	270

Oils	Tablespoons	Milliliters
Olive	4	60

Spices	Teaspoons	Milliliters
Turmeric	1	5
Coriander	1 1/2	7

Try with Example Meal 5 (Chapter 9)

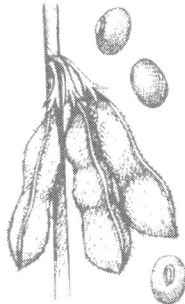

Black Cardamom (Using Dried Beans)

If you are using dried beans use the table below. Refer to chapters 3 and 5 for the method.

Bean Type	English Ounces	Metric Grams
Black	4 1/4	120

Oils	Tablespoons	Milliliters
Olive	4	60

Spices	Teaspoons	Milliliters
Turmeric	1	5
Cumin	1/2	2
Cardamom	1/2	2
Thyme	1	5

Try with Example Meal 6 (Chapter 9)

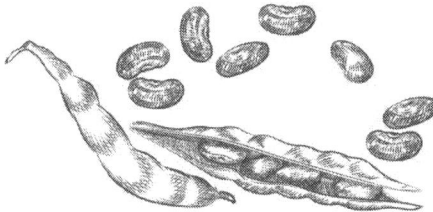

Black Cardamom (Using Canned Beans)

If you are using canned beans use the table below. Refer to chapters 4 and 5 for the method.

Bean Type	English Ounces	Metric Grams
Black (No Liquid)	9 5/8	270

Oils	Tablespoons	Milliliters
Olive	4	60

Spices	Teaspoons	Milliliters
Turmeric	1	5
Cumin	1/2	2
Cardamom	1/2	2
Thyme	1	5

Try with Example Meal 6 (Chapter 9)

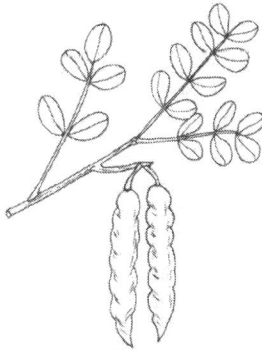

Lentil Clove (Using Dried Beans)

If you are using dried beans use the table below. Refer to chapters 3 and 5 for the method.

Bean Type	English Ounces	Metric Grams
Split Pea	1 3/4	50
Green Lentil	2 1/2	70

Oils	Tablespoons	Milliliters
Sunflower	4	60

Spices	Teaspoons	Milliliters
Clove (ground)	1/2	2
Turmeric	1/2	2
Cumin	1	5

Try with Example Meal 9 (Chapter 9)

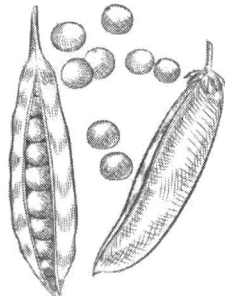

Lentil Clove (Using Canned Beans)

If you are using canned beans use the table below. Refer to chapters 4 and 5 for the method.

Bean Type	English Ounces	Metric Grams
Split Pea (No Liquid)	4	110
Green lentil (No Liquid)	5 1/2	160

Oils	Tablespoons	Milliliters
Sunflower	4	60

Spices	Teaspoons	Milliliters
Clove (ground)	1/2	2
Turmeric	1/2	2
Cumin	1	5

Try with Example Meal 9 (Chapter 9)

Cannellini Rosemary (Using Dried Beans)

If you are using dried beans use the table below. Refer to chapters 3 and 5 for the method.

Bean Type	English Ounces	Metric Grams
Cannellini	1 3/4	50
Black	1 3/8	40
Kidney	1	30

Oils	Tablespoons	Milliliters
Sesame	2	30
Olive	2	30

Spices	Teaspoons	Milliliters
Turmeric	1	5
Rosemary	1 1/2	7
Marjoram	1/2	2

Try with Example Meal 8 (Chapter 9)

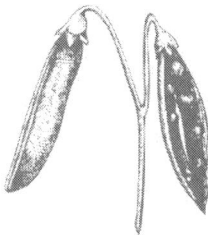

Cannellini Rosemary (Using Canned Beans)

If you are using canned beans use the table below. Refer to chapters 4 and 5 for the method.

Bean Type	English Ounces	Metric Grams
Cannellini (No Liquid)	4	110
Black (No Liquid)	3	90
Kidney (No Liquid)	2 1/2	70

Oils	Tablespoons	Milliliters
Sesame	2	30
Olive	2	30

Spices	Teaspoons	Milliliters
Turmeric	1	5
Rosemary	1 1/2	7
Marjoram	1/2	2

Try with Example Meal 8 (Chapter 9)

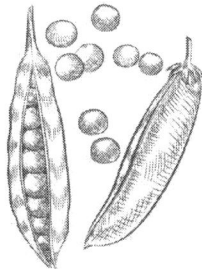

Garbanzo Rosemary (Using Dried Beans)

If you are using dried beans use the table below. Refer to chapters 3 and 5 for the method.

Bean Type	English Ounces	Metric Grams
Kidney	1	30
Garbanzo	2 1/2	70
Green Lentil	3/4	20

Oils	Tablespoons	Milliliters
Safflower	4	60

Spices	Teaspoons	Milliliters
Turmeric	1	5
Rosemary	2	10
Oregano	1	5
Basil	1	5

Try with Example Meal 6 (Chapter 9)

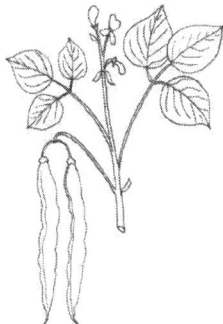

Garbanzo Rosemary (Using Canned Beans)

If you are using canned beans use the table below. Refer to chapters 4 and 5 for the method.

Bean Type	English Ounces	Metric Grams
Kidney (No Liquid)	2 3/8	70
Garbanzo (No Liquid)	5 1/2	160
Green lentil (No Liquid)	1 5/8	50

Oils	Tablespoons	Milliliters
Safflower	4	60

Spices	Teaspoons	Milliliters
Turmeric	1	5
Rosemary	2	10
Oregano	1	5
Basil	1	5

Try with Example Meal 6 (Chapter 9)

Cannellini Basil (Using Dried Beans)

If you are using dried beans use the table below. Refer to chapters 3 and 5 for the method.

Bean Type	English Ounces	Metric Grams
Cannellini	2 3/4	80
Green Lentil	1 1/2	40

Oils	Tablespoons	Milliliters
Olive	4	60

Spices	Teaspoons	Milliliters
Turmeric	1	5
Basil	2	10
Coriander	1	5

Try with Example Meal 1 (Chapter 9)

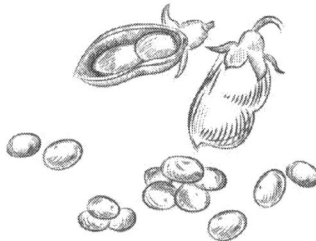

Cannellini Basil (Using Canned Beans)

If you are using canned beans use the table below. Refer to chapters 4 and 5 for the method.

Bean Type	English Ounces	Metric Grams
Cannellini (No Liquid)	6 1/4	180
Green lentil (No Liquid)	3 3/8	90

Oils	Tablespoons	Milliliters
Olive	4	60

Spices	Teaspoons	Milliliters
Turmeric	1	5
Basil	2	10
Coriander	1	5

Try with Example Meal 1 (Chapter 9)

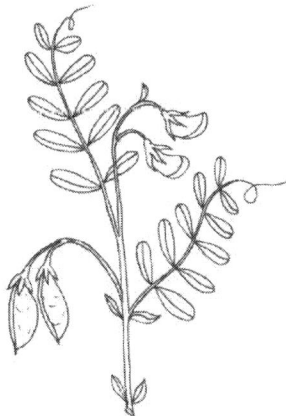

Garbanzo Pinto Basil (Using Dried Beans)

If you are using dried beans use the table below. Refer to chapters 3 and 5 for the method.

Bean Type	English Ounces	Metric Grams
Garbanzo	2 1/2	70
Black	5/8	20
Pinto	1	30

Oils	Tablespoons	Milliliters
Olive	4	60

Spices	Teaspoons	Milliliters
Turmeric	1	5
Oregano	1	5
Basil	1 1/2	7

Try with Example Meal 9 (Chapter 9)

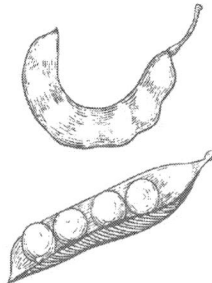

Garbanzo Pinto Basil (Using Canned Beans)

If you are using canned beans use the table below. Refer to chapters 4 and 5 for the method.

Bean Type	English Ounces	Metric Grams
Garbanzo (No Liquid)	5 1/2	160
Black (No Liquid)	2	50
Pinto (No Liquid)	2 3/8	70

Oils	Tablespoons	Milliliters
Olive	4	60

Spices	Teaspoons	Milliliters
Turmeric	1	5
Oregano	1	5
Basil	1 1/2	7

Try with Example Meal 9 (Chapter 9)

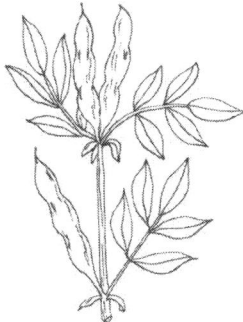

Kidney Oregano (Using Dried Beans)

If you are using dried beans use the table below. Refer to chapters 3 and 5 for the method.

Bean Type	English Ounces	Metric Grams
Kidney	2 3/4	80
Pinto	1 3/8	40

Oils	Tablespoons	Milliliters
Olive	4	60

Spices	Teaspoons	Milliliters
Turkish Oregano	2	10
Turmeric	1	5

Try with Example Meal 5 (Chapter 9)

Kidney Oregano (Using Canned Beans)

If you are using canned beans use the table below. Refer to chapters 4 and 5 for the method.

Bean Type	English Ounces	Metric Grams
Kidney (No Liquid)	6 3/8	180
Pinto (No Liquid)	3 1/4	90

Oils	Tablespoons	Milliliters
Olive	4	60

Spices	Teaspoons	Milliliters
Turkish Oregano	2	10
Turmeric	1	5

Try with Example Meal 5 (Chapter 9)

Kidney Black Cumin (Using Dried Beans)

If you are using dried beans use the table below. Refer to chapters 3 and 5 for the method.

Bean Type	English Ounces	Metric Grams
Garbanzo	3/4	20
Black	3/4	20
Pinto	3/4	20
Kidney	2	60

Oils	Tablespoons	Milliliters
Sesame	4	60

Spices	Teaspoons	Milliliters
Turmeric	1/2	2
Cumin	1	5
Cardamom	1/2	2

Try with Example Meal 4 (Chapter 9)

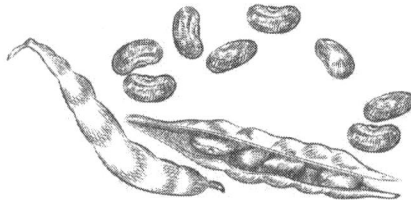

Kidney Black Cumin (Using Canned Beans)

If you are using canned beans use the table below. Refer to chapters 4 and 5 for the method.

Bean Type	English Ounces	Metric Grams
Garbanzo (No Liquid)	1 5/8	50
Black (No Liquid)	1 5/8	50
Pinto (No Liquid)	1 5/8	50
Kidney (No Liquid)	5	140

Oils	Tablespoons	Milliliters
Sesame	4	60

Spices	Teaspoons	Milliliters
Turmeric	1/2	2
Cumin	1	5
Cardamom	1/2	2

Try with Example Meal 4 (Chapter 9)

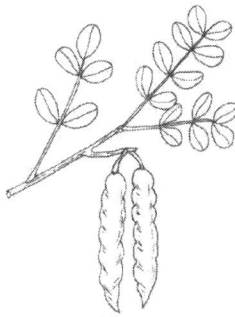

Lima Basil (Using Dried Beans)

If you are using dried beans use the table below. Refer to chapters 3 and 5 for the method.

Bean Type	English Ounces	Metric Grams
Lima	2 1/2	70
Pinto	1	30
Kidney	3/4	20

Oils	Tablespoons	Milliliters
Sesame	2	30
Olive	2	30
Coconut	1	15

Spices	Teaspoons	Milliliters
Turmeric	1	5
Basil	2	10
Nutmeg	1	5
Cumin	1 1/2	7

Try with Example Meal 3 (Chapter 9)

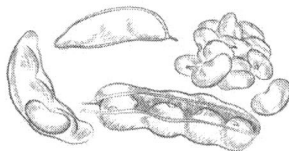

Lima Basil (Using Canned Beans)

If you are using canned beans use the table below. Refer to chapters 4 and 5 for the method.

Bean Type	English Ounces	Metric Grams
Lima (No Liquid)	5 1/2	160
Pinto (No Liquid)	2 3/8	70
Kidney (No Liquid)	1 5/8	50

Oils	Tablespoons	Milliliters
Sesame	2	30
Olive	2	30
Coconut	1	15

Spices	Teaspoons	Milliliters
Turmeric	1	5
Basil	2	10
Nutmeg	1	5
Cumin	1 1/2	7

Try with Example Meal 3 (Chapter 9)

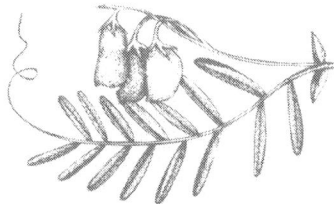

Kidney Rosemary (Using Dried Beans)

If you are using dried beans use the table below. Refer to chapters 3 and 5 for the method.

Bean Type	English Ounces	Metric Grams
Kidney	2 1/2	70
Garbanzo	1 3/4	50

Oils	Tablespoons	Milliliters
Olive	4	60

Spices	Teaspoons	Milliliters
Turmeric	1	5
Rosemary	2	10
Tarragon	1	5
Cinnamon	1/2	2

Try with Example Meal 7 (Chapter 9)

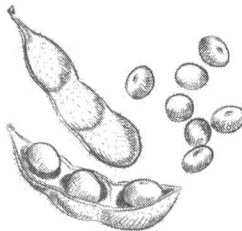

Kidney Rosemary (Using Canned Beans)

If you are using canned beans use the table below. Refer to chapters 4 and 5 for the method.

Bean Type	English Ounces	Metric Grams
Kidney (No Liquid)	5 1/2	160
Garbanzo (No Liquid)	4	110

Oils	Tablespoons	Milliliters
Olive	4	60

Spices	Teaspoons	Milliliters
Turmeric	1	5
Rosemary	2	10
Tarragon	1	5
Cinnamon	1/2	2

Try with Example Meal 7 (Chapter 9)

Pinto Dill (Using Dried Beans)

If you are using dried beans use the table below. Refer to chapters 3 and 5 for the method.

Bean Type	English Ounces	Metric Grams
Pinto	2 1/2	70
Black	1	30
Split Pea	3/4	20

Oils	Tablespoons	Milliliters
Olive	4	60

Spices	Teaspoons	Milliliters
Turmeric	1	5
Clove (ground)	1/2	2
Dillweed	1	5
Oregano	1	5

Try with Example Meal 2 (Chapter 9)

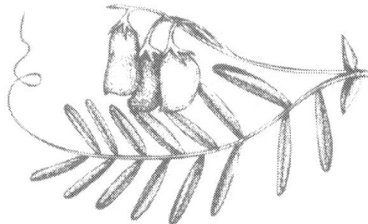

Pinto Dill (Using Canned Beans)

If you are using canned beans use the table below. Refer to chapters 4 and 5 for the method.

Bean Type	English Ounces	Metric Grams
Pinto (No Liquid)	5 1/2	160
Black (No Liquid)	2 3/8	70
Split Pea (No Liquid)	1 5/8	50

Oils	Tablespoons	Milliliters
Olive	4	60

Spices	Teaspoons	Milliliters
Turmeric	1	5
Clove (ground)	1/2	2
Dillweed	1	5
Oregano	1	5

Try with Example Meal 2 (Chapter 9)

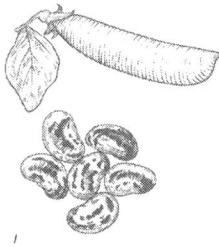

Cannellini Tarragon (Using Dried Beans)

If you are using dried beans use the table below. Refer to chapters 3 and 5 for the method.

Bean Type	English Ounces	Metric Grams
Cannellini	2	60
Black	1	30
Garbanzo	1	30

Oils	Tablespoons	Milliliters
Grape Seed	4	60
Coconut	1	15

Spices	Teaspoons	Milliliters
Turmeric	1	5
Tarragon	1 1/2	7
Coriander	1	5

Try with Example Meal 10 (Chapter 9)

Cannellini Tarragon (Using Canned Beans)

If you are using canned beans use the table below. Refer to chapters 4 and 5 for the method.

Bean Type	English Ounces	Metric Grams
Cannellini (No Liquid)	5	140
Black (No Liquid)	2 3/8	70
Garbanzo (No Liquid)	2 3/8	70

Oils	Tablespoons	Milliliters
Grapeseed	4	60
Coconut	1	15

Spices	Teaspoons	Milliliters
Turmeric	1	5
Tarragon	1 1/2	7
Coriander	1	5

Try with Example Meal 10 (Chapter 9)

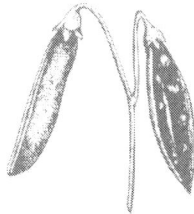

Pinto Black Basil (Using Dried Beans)

If you are using dried beans use the table below. Refer to chapters 3 and 5 for the method.

Bean Type	English Ounces	Metric Grams
Pinto	2	60
Black	1 3/8	40
Green Lentil	3/4	20

Oils	Tablespoons	Milliliters
Grape Seed	4	60

Spices	Teaspoons	Milliliters
Turmeric	1	5
Basil	1 1/2	7
Rosemary	1	5

Try with Example Meal 8 (Chapter 9)

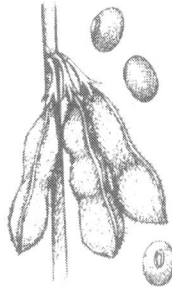

Pinto Black Basil (Using Canned Beans)

If you are using canned beans use the table below. Refer to chapters 4 and 5 for the method.

Bean Type	English Ounces	Metric Grams
Pinto (No Liquid)	5	140
Black (No Liquid)	3	90
Green Lentil (No Liquid)	1 5/8	50

Oils	Tablespoons	Milliliters
Grapeseed	4	60

Spices	Teaspoons	Milliliters
Turmeric	1	5
Basil	1 1/2	7
Rosemary	1	5

Try with Example Meal 8 (Chapter 9)

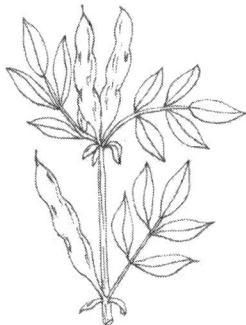

7 SERVING AND VARIATIONS

If desired you can use the sauce immediately after blending. Over meals you will find they work best served warm or hot. You can use them over rice, chicken or beef, or a bed of vegetables. One of my favorite servings for the sauces is to make a medley of the meat, rice and vegetables and spoon the sauce over the top (see front cover). In Chapter 9 you will find some of these meal suggestions to use with the sauces.

Variations
1) You can also use these sauces served cold as a vegetable dip, chip dip or with cheese and crackers. You can use cayenne pepper, garlic or ginger to spice them up.

2) You will find some delightful surprises using fresh chopped garlic or ginger over the top. They both go very well with most of the sauces.

3) You may also like to try adding your favorite cheese to top off the sauces as well. Fresh spaghetti cheese over the top will spice these up nicely.

4) Cayenne pepper is also highly recommended. If you are adding this to the whole sauce (2 ½ cups) add it in about 1/8 teaspoon at a time. Mix the sauce thoroughly and taste after each addition. To be conservative you can add the cayenne pepper at serving time.

5) I prefer adding salt at serving time. Many salts are available and each will give a different texture and taste. Kosher and sea salts are my favorites.

You may wish to taste test a small amount of the sauce with your chosen added toppings before serving. These sauces go with many meal types so experiment and enjoy!

8 SAUCE STORAGE

In general, these sauces will keep in the refrigerator for about 2 to 4 days depending on the freshness of ingredients and how they are handled. It is okay to freeze them as well. In both cases make sure they are in a sealed container preferably glass. Sometimes these sauces can leach a plastic taste from a plastic container.

These sauces go very well with things like fresh ginger and garlic. But mixing fresh ginger and or garlic within the sauce and storing it that way is not a good idea. For some reason, it spoils or some chemistry takes over that ruins the taste. If you wish to use fresh plant-based spices, it is best to put them on the sauce at the time of serving.

These sauces are also complemented by cheeses. But again, it is not a good idea for you to mix them into the sauce and store them that way. Always put cheeses on at the time of serving.

If you choose you can make your sauce spicy hot with cayenne pepper. This one is the exception and can be stored mixed into the sauce.

In general, do not add anything extra to the sauce if you are going to store it in the refrigerator or freezer. Also, if you are using fresh spices it is best to use the sauce immediately and not store it.

If storing the sauce, you may notice that it sometimes matures and gets better after a day or so as the flavors are allowed to merge more thoroughly.

9 EXAMPLE MEALS FOR THE SAUCES

If you are not sure how to use these sauces you can choose from any of the tried and true 10 meal plans shown in this chapter. Here you will find some of the ingredients that I use most often and how they can be combined into meals. Notice that in these recipes you will not find amounts. That part is left up to you.

I normally prepare the ingredients in a salad and ladle the sauce over the top (similar to what is shown on the front cover).

Cook the rice, potatoes and meat to your desired liking. The other vegetables can be left raw or lightly cooked.

If you would like a suggestion for a single serving meal you can follow these general guidelines.

a) 20 to 35 g of rice dry   or   40 to 60 g of fresh potato
b) 60 to 85 g of meat
c) 20 to 35 g of each vegetable

Over the top add 2 to 4 tablespoons of the sauce.

Meal Plan 1

Starch

Rice White Basmati

Meat

Chicken Breast

Vegetables

Kale Green Curly
Squash Yellow
Tomato Beefsteak
Mushrooms White Button
Onion White
Bell Pepper Orange

Meal Plan 2

Starch

Rice Yellow Basmati

Meat

Chicken Breast

Vegetables

Kale Russian
Cucumber
Avocado
Onion Yellow
Bell Pepper Red

Meal Plan 3

Starch
Rice White Basmati

Meat
Chicken Thighs

Vegetables
Kale Lacinato
Zucchini Green
Tomato Cherry
Onion Red
Bell Pepper Orange

Meal Plan 4

Starch
Potato Redskin

Meat
Lean Beef

Vegetables
Kale Redbor
Squash Yellow
Tomato Beefsteak
Mushrooms Crimini
Onion Red
Bell Pepper Green

Meal Plan   5

Starch
Rice White Basmati

Meat
Chicken Breast

Vegetables
Kale Green Curly
Zucchini Green
Tomato Roma
Avocado
Onion Scallion
Bell Pepper Orange

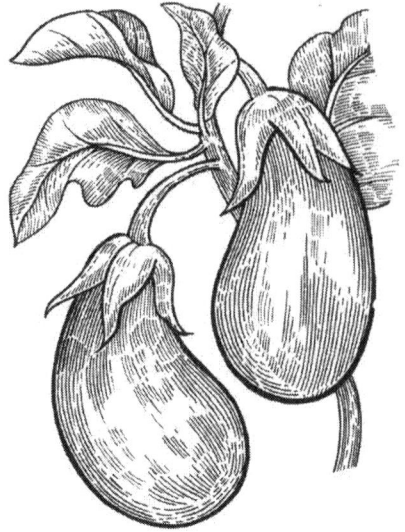

Meal Plan   6

Starch
Rice Yellow Basmati

Meat
Lean Beef

Vegetables
Spinach
Squash Yellow
Tomato Cherry
Mushrooms White Button
Onion Yellow
Bell Pepper Green

Meal Plan 7

Starch

Potato Sweet

Meat

Chicken Breast

Vegetables

Kale Lacinato
Cucumber
Tomato Beefsteak
Mushrooms Crimini
Onion Yellow
Bell Pepper Yellow

Meal Plan 8

Starch

Rice White Jasmine

Meat

Chicken Thighs

Vegetables

Dandelion Greens
Zucchini Green
Tomato Roma
Onion White
Bell Pepper Green

Meal Plan   9

Starch

Rice Yellow Basmati

Meat

Chicken Breast

Vegetables

Kale Green Curly
Zucchini Green
Avocado
Onion Red
Bell Pepper Yellow

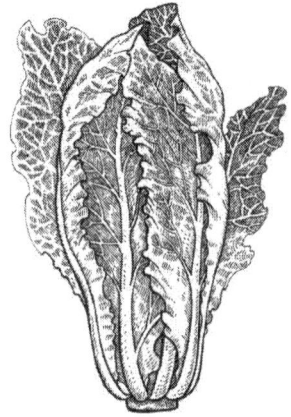

Meal Plan   10

Starch

Rice White Basmati

Meat

Chicken Breast

Vegetables

Kale Redbor
Squash Yellow
Tomato Beefsteak
Onion White
Bell Pepper Green

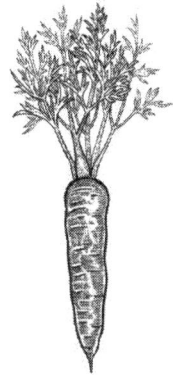

10 FOOD INDEX

Avocado Oil.. 34, 68, 70, 72
Basil...26, 30, 32, 44, 46, 48, 54, 62
Beef... 69, 70
Bell Pepper Green... 69, 70, 71, 72
Bell Pepper Orange... 68, 69, 70
Bell Pepper Red 68
Bell Pepper Yellow... 71, 72
Black Beans 34, 38, 42, 48, 52, 58, 60, 62
Cannellini 36, 42, 46, 60
Cardamom 38, 52
Chicken Breast 68, 70, 71, 72
Chicken Thighs 69, 71
Cinnamon... 56
Clove 30, 40, 58
Coconut Oil 30, 54, 60
Coriander 26, 28, 32, 36, 46, 60
Cucumber 68, 71
Cumin... 24, 28, 38, 40, 52, 54
Dandelion Greens 71
Dillweed... 58
Garbanzo 26, 30, 34, 44, 48, 52, 56, 60
Grape Seed Oil 28, 60, 62
Green Lentil 28, 40, 44, 46, 62
Kale Green Curly 68, 70, 72
Kale Lacinato.. 69, 71
Kale Redbor 69, 72
Kale Russian 68
Kidney 24, 42, 44, 50, 52, 54, 56
Lima 54
Marjoram.. 24, 34, 42
Mushrooms Crimini 69, 71
Mushrooms White Button... 68, 70
Mustard 32
Nutmeg 54
Olive Oil 26, 30, 36, 38, 42, 46, 48, 50, 54, 56, 58
Onion Red 69, 72
Onion Scallion 70

Onion White 68, 71, 72
Onion Yellow 68, 70, 71
Oregano 34, 44, 48, 50, 58
Pinto 32, 48, 50, 52, 54, 58, 62
Potato Redskin.. 69
Potato Sweet 71
Rice White Basmati 68, 69, 70, 72
Rice White Jasmine... 71
Rice Yellow Basmati... 68, 70, 72
Rosemary...32, 42, 44, 56, 62
Safflower Oil 32, 44
Sesame Oil 24, 28, 42, 52, 54
Spinnach 70
Split Pea 40, 58
Squash Yellow...68, 69, 70, 72
Sunflower OIl 40
Tarragon 34, 56, 60
Thyme.. 24, 38
Tomato Beefsteak 68, 69, 71, 72
Tomato Cherry... 69, 70
Tomato Roma 70, 71
Turkish Oregano 50
Turmeric . 24, 26, 28, 30, 32, 34, 36, 38, 40, 42, 44, 46, 48, 50, 52, 54, 56, 58, 60, 62
Zucchini Green...69, 70, 71, 72

ABOUT THE AUTHOR

I love cooking and am always looking for healthy and easier ways to cook. The sauce development and documentation process has been an exciting and rewarding 5 year journey.

I was a mechanical engineer for 34 years but am now retired so I have time to cook and write more. My work years were split between mechanical design, lab measurement work and finally computer simulation. During this time, I also received two United States patents.

To date, I have been playing guitar for 44 years and violin for about 25. Since I have recently retired I am now teaching guitar as well as performing.

For health reasons I became a yoga teacher; I teach weekly at a facility that works with troubled teenagers. I have been teaching at the same facility since 2001. My estimates show that I have introduced yoga to about 2600 teens.

38180007R00048

Made in the USA
Columbia, SC
03 December 2018